My First
REFERENCE LIBRARY

The World of
ANIMALS

V. HARRISON
S. POLLOCK

Gareth Stevens Children's Books
MILWAUKEE

For a free color catalog describing Gareth Stevens' list of high-quality children's books call 1-800-341-3569

Library of Congress Cataloging-in-Publication Data
Harrison, Virginia, 1966-
    The world of animals / by Virginia Harrison and Steve Pollock.
      p. cm. — (My first reference library)

    Includes index.
    Summary: A survey of the characteristics, habits, and natural environment
of animals from all over the world. Also introduces the scientific grouping
and classification of animal life.
    ISBN 0-8368-0028-1
    1. Animals—Juvenile literature. 2. Zoology—Classification—Juvenile literature.
[1. Animals. 2. Zoology—Classification.] I. Pollock, Steve (Stephen Thomas) II. Title.
III. Series.
QL49.H334   1989
591—dc20   89-11357

North American edition first published in 1990 by
Gareth Stevens, Inc.
RiverCenter Building, Suite 201
1555 North RiverCenter Drive
Milwaukee, Wisconsin 53212, USA

Photographic credits: Bruce Coleman, pp. 26, 36 (right), 37, 52; Frank Lane, pp. 15, 18 (right),
25, 30, 32-34, 36 (left), 38, 40, 43, 45, 46, 48, 49, 53, 55-59; Natural Science Photos, pp. 18 (left),
19 (right); NHPA, p. 27; Oxford Scientific Films, pp. 31, 39; Planet Earth, pp. 9, 58

Illustrated by Adam Abel, Teresa O'Brien, Eric Robson, Roger Walker, and Lorna Turpin

Cover illustration © Jerry Gadamus, 1989,
courtesy of Northwoods Craftsman, Menomonee Falls, WI

Series editors: Mark Sachner and Neil Champion
Research editor: Scott Enk
Educational consultant: Dr. Alistair Ross
Editorial consultant: Neil Morris
Design: Groom and Pickerill
Picture research and art editing: Ann Usborne
Specialist consultant: the late Dr. Gwynne Vevers

Printed in the United States of America

1 2 3 4 5 6 7 8 9 96 95 94 93 92 91 90

Contents

1: ANIMAL LIFE

The Animal Kingdom

All animals eat, drink, and breathe. They also have the senses of sight, hearing, touch, taste, and smell. These senses help them find food and shelter.

Animals Everywhere

Animals adapt to almost every place in the world. They may live in trees or on the ground, on the plains or in the forests, in the deserts or in the oceans.

Penguins have adapted to their life in Antarctic waters. Their wings have become flippers, so instead of flying, they swim. The

Temperate Woodland

Fox

Rabbits

Beetle

A Hot African Desert

Fennec fox

Jerboa

penguin also has a sharp beak for grabbing its fish prey.

The Variety of Animal Life

Today we know of about a million different kinds, or species, of animals. Hundreds of new species are discovered each year. But many species are destroyed by humans before they can even be found.

All living things depend on other living and nonliving things. Animals feed on plants or other animals. They also depend on nonliving things such as oxygen, water, and sunlight.

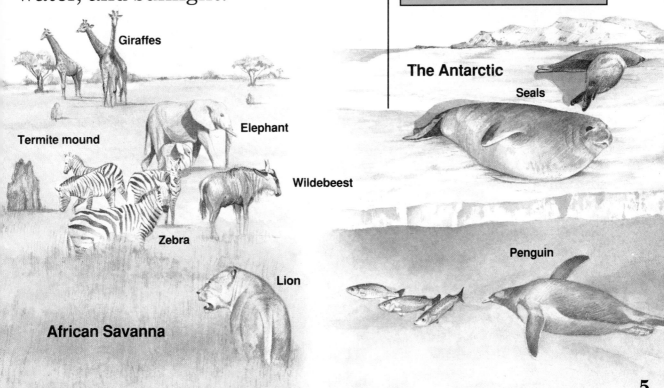

Giraffes

Termite mound

Elephant

Wildebeest

Zebra

Lion

African Savanna

The Antarctic

Seals

Penguin

Animal Groups

1 The lion is a big cat. All big cats roar and leave their feet unfolded in front of them. Lions and other big cats are in a group, or genus. The big cat genus is called *Panthera*, and the scientific names of all big cats begin with *Panthera*.

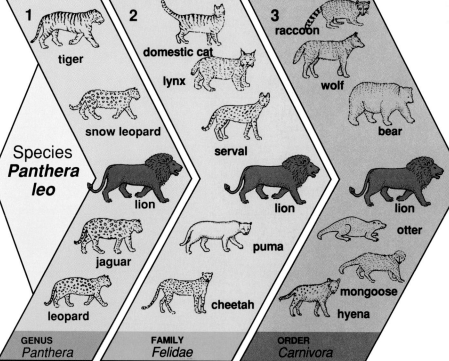

1	2	3
tiger	domestic cat	raccoon
snow leopard	lynx	wolf
Species *Panthera leo*	serval	bear
lion	lion	lion
jaguar	puma	otter
leopard	cheetah	mongoose / hyena
GENUS *Panthera*	**FAMILY** *Felidae*	**ORDER** *Carnivora*

▲

It helps our understanding of animal groups to look at one animal, the lion. The lion has features that no other animal has, so biologists have named it and put it into a group by itself. This group is called a species. Biologists named the lion *Panthera leo*, and it is the only animal with this name.

2 Big and little cats share some features, so they are put into a group called a family. The cat family includes all breeds of cat, both large and small. It includes the lynx, the domestic cat, the lion, the puma, and the cheetah. Biologists have named the cat family *Felidae*.

3 As meat-eaters, cats have teeth similar to other meat-eaters such as the dog, bear, and raccoon families. These animals are put into the next group, called an order. Biologists have named the meat-eating order of animals *Carnivora*. We call meat-eating animals carnivores.

4 Several orders make up the next group, called a class. Each animal in this class has hair, gives birth to live young in most cases, and feeds its young on the milk of the mother. The animals in this class are called *Mammalia*. Humans are mammals.

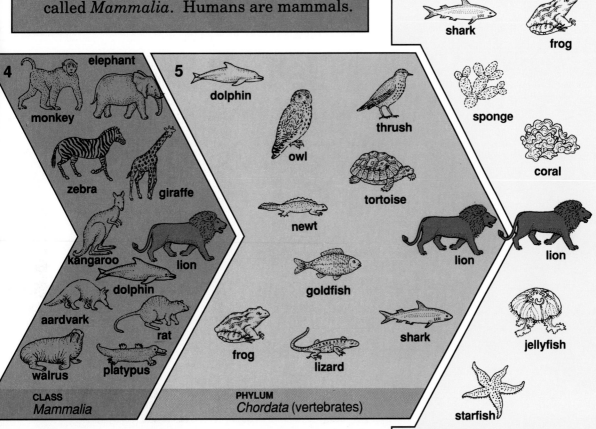

CLASS
Mammalia

PHYLUM
Chordata (vertebrates)

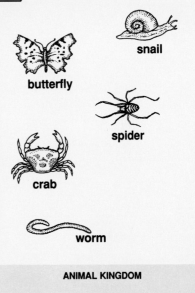

ANIMAL KINGDOM

5 Many classes make up the next group, a phylum. This phylum, called the *Chordata*, includes vertebrates (animals with a backbone), and protochordates (not shown here). Vertebrates are familiar to us and include fish, reptiles, amphibians, birds, and mammals.

6 The last group is the Animal Kingdom. All animals are included here: 45,000 different vertebrates and 950,000 different invertebrates (animals without backbones). A kingdom is the largest group of living things. There are other kingdoms, too — the Plant Kingdom, for example.

Animal Evolution

After millions of years, most animals of today are different from their ancestors. Over time, some animals may change into new species. Others may die out and become extinct.

The Dinosaurs

Dinosaurs lived millions of years ago for about 140 million years. Some, like Diplodocus, were as big as three semitrailer trucks.

**Tyrannosaurus rex
(90 million years ago)**

Pteranodon — flying reptile (90 million years ago)

Diplodocus (140 million years ago)

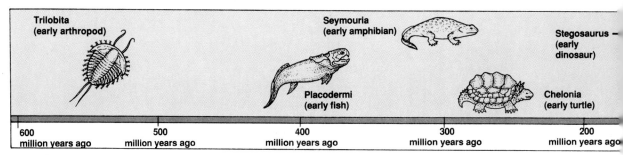

Trilobita
(early arthropod)

Seymouria
(early amphibian)

Stegosaurus —
(early
dinosaur)

Placodermi
(early fish)

Chelonia
(early turtle)

600 million years ago	500 million years ago	400 million years ago	300 million years ago	200 million years ago

They all became extinct about 65 million years ago.

The Record in the Rocks
We learn about extinct species by studying fossilized bones, teeth, and shells. These remains become rock while buried for millions of years.

Life on Earth began in the sea 3.5 billion years ago. Early fish, the first animals with backbones, appeared 500 million years ago. These animals have evolved, or changed, over many years.

Living Fossils ▲
This primitive fish, called a coelacanth, was believed to have been extinct for 70 million years. But in 1938 a living one was taken from the deep sea. It probably stayed the same all that time because its deep-sea surroundings had not changed much.

◄ **Time Line:** This time line shows when certain forms of life, including an ancestor of human beings, first appeared on Earth.

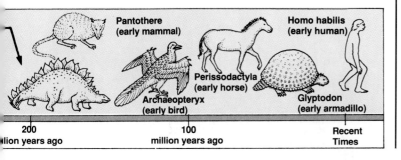

Pantothere
(early mammal)

Homo habilis
(early human)

Perissodactyla
(early horse)

Archaeopteryx
(early bird)

Glyptodon
(early armadillo)

200
million years ago

100
million years ago

Recent
Times

Breathing

Caterpillar

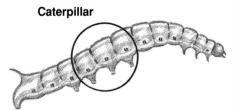

Spiracles

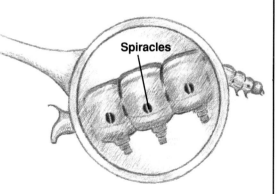

▲An insect breathes through holes on the side of its body. The holes are called spiracles.

Did You Know?

The lungfish from Africa can breathe in water and in the air. This fish wraps itself in a cocoon of slime. It can live like this until the next rains fill the lakes. This could be years!

The dolphin. Like humans, the dolphin is a mammal. It breathes through lungs and has to hold its breath when it is underwater.

In order to live, all animals must breathe in oxygen and breathe out carbon dioxide. Some animals breathe oxygen from the air. Others breathe oxygen from the water.

Breathing in Air

Air-breathers, such as insects, birds, and mammals, get oxygen from the air they breathe. An earthworm can breathe through its skin. This is called diffusion. Larger animals have lungs and need special breathing systems.

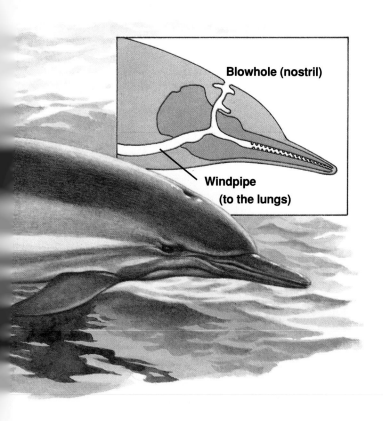

Blowhole (nostril)

Windpipe
(to the lungs)

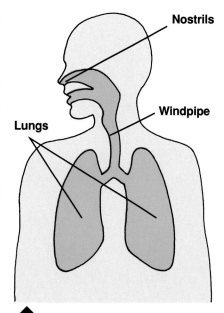

Nostrils

Windpipe

Lungs

▲
People and dolphins use lungs to breathe. Air passes in and out of the body through the nostrils. Dolphins' nostrils are on top of their heads.

Breathing in Water

Animals that breathe under water use gills. As lungs do with air, gills absorb oxygen from the water.

Some animals live in water but breathe air. Dolphins and whales are air-breathing mammals. Their nostril, called a blowhole, is on top of their heads. When a whale surfaces, it blows out its breath through the blowhole.

The fish breathes in water through its mouth and out its gill flaps. Blood vessels in the gills take out the oxygen and carry it through the fish's body.

▼

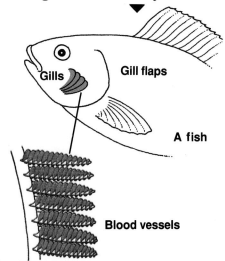

Gills

Gill flaps

A fish

Blood vessels

Hot and Cold Animals

Warm Blood, Cold Blood

Warm-blooded animals have warm body temperatures that don't change much. Cold-blooded animals have body temperatures that change with the air temperature. Birds and mammals, including humans, are warm-blooded. Birds have feathers and most mammals have fur to help keep heat in their bodies. Cold-blooded animals, including invertebrates, fish, amphibians, and reptiles, cannot keep a constant body

Fur   Blubber

Skin

Muscle

Some Warm-blooded Animals

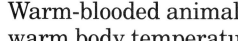

Dolphin

Bat

Penguin

Tarsier

Deer

Pigeon

Polar bear

Shrew

temperature the way warm-blooded animals can, so they must avoid extreme heat or cold.

Getting Away from It All

To protect themselves from the cold of winter, some mammals add more fat layers and go into hibernation until the spring comes. Some birds migrate to warmer places to avoid the cold. Some cold-blooded animals, such as lizards, snakes, and frogs, also hibernate, the way warm-blooded mammals do.

Warm-blooded animals:
• Have feathers or fur to keep them warm.
• Body temperature stays the same most of the time.
• They rely on food to make their body heat.

Cold-blooded animals:
• Have no special skin covering to stay warm.
• Use heat from the Sun to keep up body heat.

Some Cold-blooded Animals

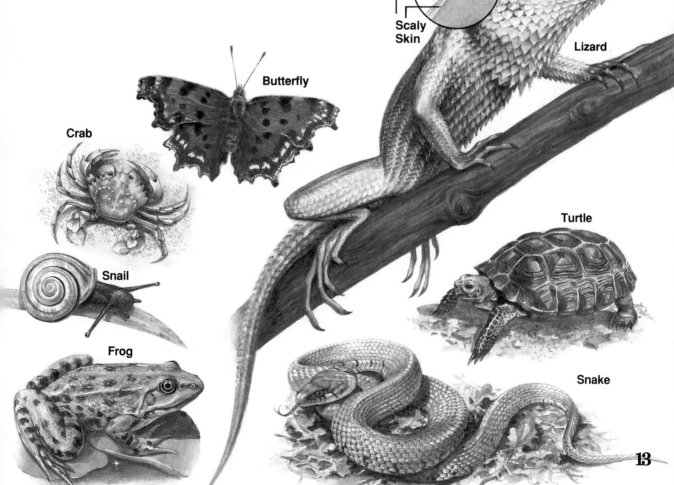

Muscle

Scaly Skin

Lizard

Butterfly

Crab

Turtle

Snail

Frog

Snake

2: | MOVEMENT

Moving on Land

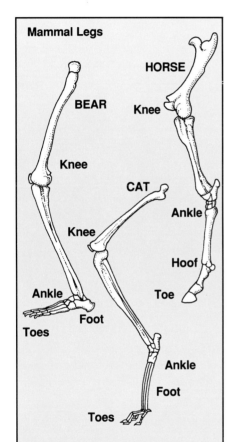

Mammal Legs

HORSE

BEAR

Knee

Knee

CAT

Ankle

Knee

Hoof

Ankle

Toe

Foot

Toes

Ankle

Foot

Toes

The bones of these three animals are each built to move at different speeds. The slow bear puts its whole foot on the ground. The faster cat puts part of its foot on the ground. The horse puts only its toenail on the ground.

Land animals get support for their bodies from their limbs and skeletons. Humans have two legs, cats have four legs — some animals have hundreds of legs! Not all land animals have legs. Snakes and some lizards wriggle their bodies and press against the ground. Muscles use energy to move the bones, which in turn move the animal.

Supporting Skeletons
The animals we have talked

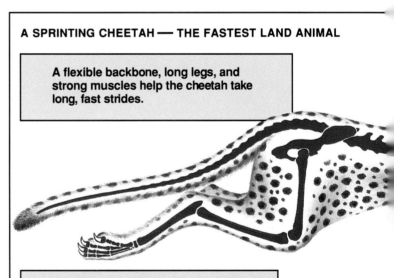

A SPRINTING CHEETAH — THE FASTEST LAND ANIMAL

A flexible backbone, long legs, and strong muscles help the cheetah take long, fast strides.

Unlike other cats, the cheetah keeps its claws out for gripping like spikes on athletic shoes.

about here are vertebrates. They have bony skeletons <u>inside</u> their bodies. Invertebrates have a skeleton or shell on the <u>outside</u> of their bodies. Both groups of animals use muscles to move.

Fast Runners

Animals need long legs and a small amount of contact with the ground to run fast. The cheetah has long legs and touches only part of its clawed foot to the ground. Its long tail helps it balance. The cheetah is the fastest land animal, reaching a top speed of 70 miles (112 km) per hour over short distances.

▲ Crabs' skeletons are outside their bodies. Two of their legs are pincers, which they use to defend themselves.

Facts & Feats

• The South African sharp-nosed frog jumps farther than any other frog. A female jumped 9 feet 10 inches (3 m).

• An ostrich has only two toes on each foot. It can run up to 40 miles (64 km) an hour.

• The fastest land animal is the cheetah, known to run up to 70 miles (112 km) an hour.

• The common garden snail has a top speed of 52.8 yards (47.5 m) an hour. This means that it would take a snail more than 33 hours to travel one mile (about 2/3 km). The cheetah could run this far in just over 50 seconds!

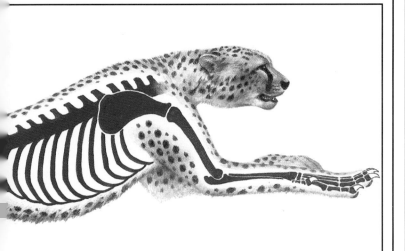

Hard footpads have ridges that act like tire treads to give extra grip.

15

Moving in Trees

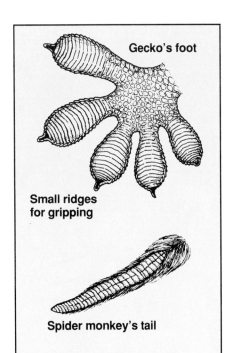

Gecko's foot

Small ridges for gripping

Spider monkey's tail

Did You Know?

The bottom of the toes of tree frogs and some lizards are swollen with tiny ridges and hooks. These special toes allow the animals to grip onto shiny surfaces by hooking into tiny cracks in the surface. They can even hang from glass!

To move in trees without falling, an animal needs a tight grip, good eyesight to judge distance, and a way to balance itself.

The Graspers

Humans, monkeys, and apes have hands that grasp. We have what is called an opposable thumb. Some monkeys and other tree-living animals have prehensile tails, or gripping tails. Birds grip with their feet and toes. Birds that have feet with three toes in front and one

Emerald tree boa — moves by coiling itself around branches

Tree frog — has special suckerlike toes for gripping

in back grip tree branches. Woodpeckers, which grip the <u>sides</u> of trees, have two toes in front and two in back.

Swingers, Leapers, and Balancers

Some monkeys swing through the trees using their hands to grip the branches. Squirrels leap with their strong hind legs. When they run along narrow branches or when they are landing, they use their tails to balance their weight.

Spider monkey — grips branches with extra limb, its prehensile tail

Crimson-crested woodpecker — to climb trees, grips with its claws and uses its tail for support

Tamandua (a tree-dwelling anteater) — uses prehensile tail to grip branches

Sloth — hangs upside-down using its claws like a coat hanger

Anolis lizard — uses its suckerlike toes to grip branches

17

Moving in Earth

Many animals have homes underground to protect themselves from enemies and extreme temperatures.

Tools for Digging

Burrowers have feet, claws, and bodies made for digging. Both the termite-eating aardvark from Africa and the armadillo from North and South America use their strong front legs and wide, thick claws to dig burrows.

▲ The jackknife clam uses its long, muscular foot to burrow deep in the sand.

The armadillo has strong front legs and large claws. ▶

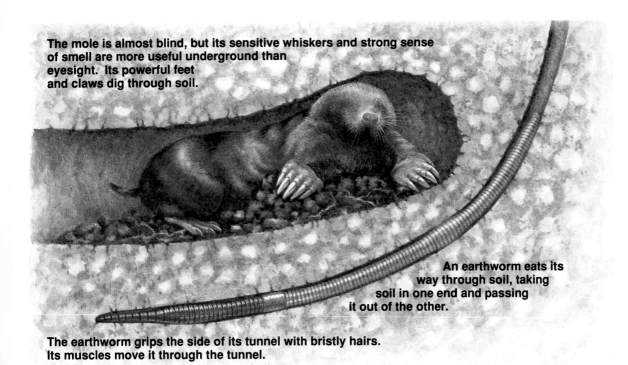

The mole is almost blind, but its sensitive whiskers and strong sense of smell are more useful underground than eyesight. Its powerful feet and claws dig through soil.

An earthworm eats its way through soil, taking soil in one end and passing it out of the other.

The earthworm grips the side of its tunnel with bristly hairs. Its muscles move it through the tunnel.

The mole has thick, wide claws, too. It also has flat, strong feet that work like shovels against the ground. Its short, slick fur moves both ways as it burrows and thus doesn't pick up dirt.

Burrowers without Backbones
Moles eat another burrower — the earthworm. Worms have tiny, bristly hairs that push their smooth bodies through the soil. They also have many segments in their bodies to help them stretch and move. And when worms get to harder soil, they simply <u>eat</u> their way through!

▲ Animals that live underground have adapted to where they live. Their special traits make them experts at what they do.

▲ The sandfish is not a fish, but a lizard. Its snakelike body helps it to "swim" through the sand.

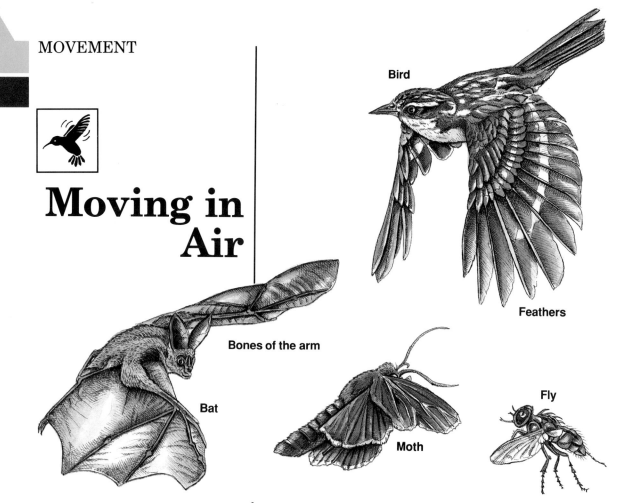

Moving in Air

Bird

Feathers

Bones of the arm

Bat

Moth

Fly

▲ To move through air, animals use wings. The bat is the only flying mammal. It has wings made of bones and thin skin. Birds have wings made of skin, bones, and feathers. All flying animals have strong muscles that make their wings beat up and down.

Did You Know?

Beetles, like other insects, have four wings. But their two outside wings are hard. Their job is to protect the two soft inside wings.

Wings

Some animals that move in the air fly, some glide, and some do both. Bats, birds, and insects fly with wide, flat wings. Most insects have two pairs of delicate wings that are made stronger by a network of veins. Birds have feathers and hollow bones, both of which make the birds light. Bats have a thin skin, or membrane, that stretches across their legs, arms, hands, and fingers.

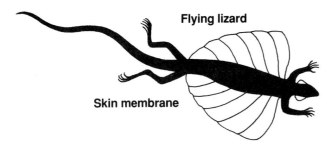

Flying lizard

Skin membrane

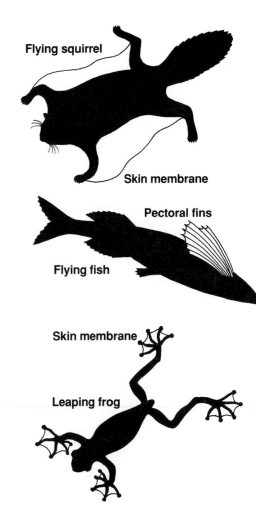

Flying squirrel

Skin membrane

Pectoral fins

Flying fish

Skin membrane

Leaping frog

Gliders

There are many kinds of gliding animals that soar on the air but cannot fly. Flying lizards, frogs, and squirrels have membranes to catch the wind and keep them up in the air. Flying fish have big pectoral fins that look like wings. These fish can leap and glide above the ocean surface for up to 1,300 feet (400 m).

▲ All of these animals are gliding animals. They soar from high to low in the air, but they cannot fly.

◀ Birds have curved wings that lift them in the air. Their strong muscles and lightweight bones also help them fly.

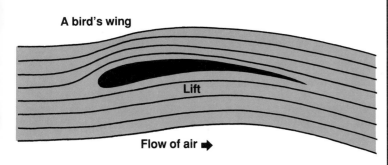

A bird's wing

Lift

Flow of air ➡

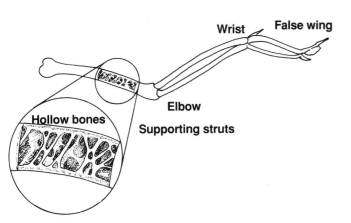

Wrist   False wing

Elbow

Hollow bones

Supporting struts

Parachuting Spiders

Some tiny spiders can release a long, silky thread that catches the wind. Like parachutes, these spiders can drift over long distances.

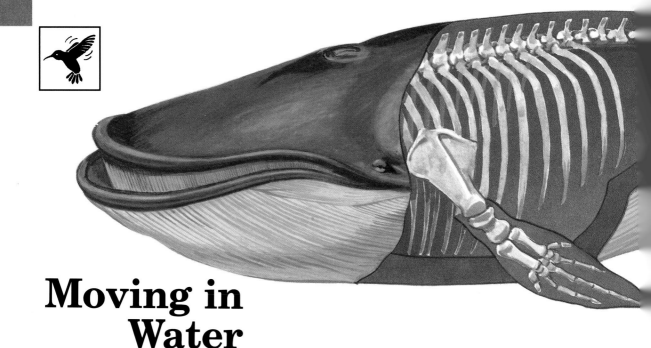

Moving in Water

These animals have a ▲ streamlined shape for moving in water. The seal and penguin use flippers to move. The pike uses its fins and tail.

We can float in water but not in air. We can do this because water is 800 times more dense, or thick, than air. The blue whale is the largest and heaviest animal that ever lived. It floats in water, but it would not be able to move on land.

Streamlining
The blue whale is an aquatic mammal. It lives in the water, but it breathes air. Like the seal, it has a streamlined body that is narrow at each end and wider in the middle.

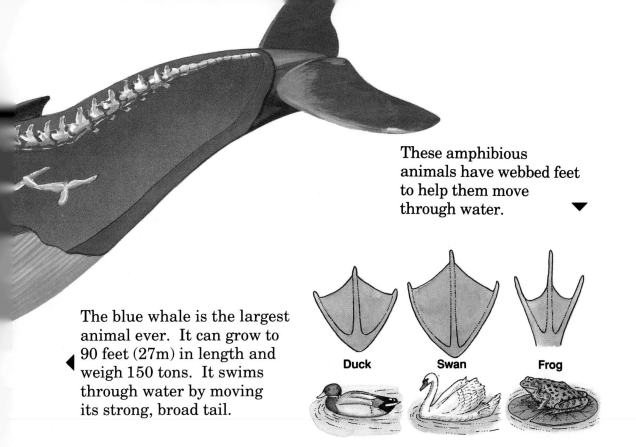

These amphibious animals have webbed feet to help them move through water. ▼

Duck   **Swan**   **Frog**

◄ The blue whale is the largest animal ever. It can grow to 90 feet (27m) in length and weigh 150 tons. It swims through water by moving its strong, broad tail.

Only the flippers and the pelvic bone remain of the ancestors of the present-day whale. Millions of years ago, the pelvic bone was attached to the back legs of whale ancestors!

Swimming Styles

Whales and most fish use their tails to swim. The coral fish has large pectoral fins that it uses to row through the water. The cuttlefish moves very fast using jet propulsion. It sucks water in and squirts it out quickly through a tube in its body.

Facts & Feats

• Grebes are aquatic birds. But unlike ducks, they have feet at the end of their bodies. This makes it hard for them to balance on land.

• The fastest-swimming mammal is the killer whale. One was clocked at 34.5 miles (55 km) per hour.

• The gray whale migrates almost 12,000 miles (20,000 km) every year from the Bering Sea to California and Mexico and back.

3: EATING AND BEING EATEN

Hunters and Killers

Predatory animals kill and eat other animals, which are called prey. Animals do this in different ways.

A Tiger Kills
The Bengal tiger stalks its prey, antelope and deer, quietly and slowly. Its sharp claws are hidden in sheaths inside its soft

Super Swallowers

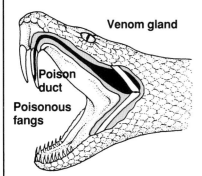

The rattlesnake catches its prey by shooting a poisonous liquid called venom into its victim. The venom comes out of hollow fangs at the front of the snake's mouth. The venom can kill a mouse or rat in a few minutes. The snake can then swallow its victim whole, and strong digestive juices break down the entire mouse or rat.

paws. When the tiger gets close enough, it rushes its prey, grips the animal with its sharp claws, and bites with its canine teeth.

Seashore Soup

The starfish is a star-shaped sea animal. It wraps its body around its prey of mussels and clams and uses its strong feet to grip their shells. It then pulls the shells open and inserts its stomach between the shells. Digestive stomach juices break down the soft part of the prey, and the starfish absorbs the "soup."

▲ The golden eagle uses its hooked beak to tear the flesh off its prey.

◀ The Bengal tiger quietly stalks its prey until it is close enough to leap on it.

Drilling for "Soup"

One kind of snail uses part of its body to drill through a mollusk's shell. The snail then pours digestive juices into the hole and sucks up the "soup."

Ambushers, Anglers, and Trappers

While many animals must chase their prey, others can wait for their live meal to come to them. These animals are specially adapted to lure or trap their prey.

Ambushers

Ambushers wait for their victim to come close to them, and then catch them suddenly. The sea anemone looks like an aquatic plant to its victims — until it strikes with its deadly tentacles. The chameleon is an ambusher which waits motionless in trees and bushes and catches insects with its long, sticky tongue.

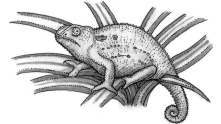

Chameleons change color to match their surroundings. This is called camouflage. Their eyes can move forward or backward independently of one another! ▲

Sea anemone

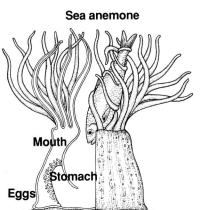

Mouth

Stomach

Eggs

This sea anemone has caught a fish with its ▲ tentacles and has stunned it with poisonous darts. It uses its tentacles to push the fish into its stomach to be digested.

Anglers and Trappers

The anglerfish and the alligator snapping turtle catch food with body parts that look like live bait. The snapping turtle has a tongue that looks like a worm. The turtle wiggles its tongue to catch curious fish. The anglerfish (above) has a long spine that dangles from its head. Some animals build traps to catch their prey. Spiders weave webs of silky thread to catch flying insects. When an insect sticks to the web, the spider feels the vibrations on the thread and rushes to bite its victim.

The anglerfish dangles ▲ its bait from its head like a fishing rod. When small fish try to eat the bait, the anglerfish opens its mouth and eats <u>them</u>.

The ant lion larva ▲ builds a sandy pit and opens its jaws wide. Ants and other small insects fall into its trap and are eaten up.

Plant Eaters

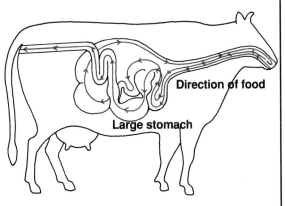

▲ The cow chews grass and swallows it. After a while, the grass comes back up, and the cow chews it again. When the cow swallows a second time, the food goes into a second part of the stomach, where it is further digested.

Direction of food

Large stomach

Did You Know?

The coconut crab goes to a lot of trouble to find its favorite food. It cannot crack coconuts open, but it looks everywhere it can for broken coconuts!

Animals that eat only plants are called herbivores. They can find food almost anywhere.

Hungry Herbivores

Plants are hard to digest and are not very nutritious foods. Therefore, animals must work hard to get as much from their food as possible. Cows, sheep, giraffes, antelope, and deer have large stomachs to hold lots of vegetation. The cow has adapted well to digesting grass. It chews grass twice and has two parts to its stomach to help digest its food. The second time it chews a mouthful, the cow is said to chew its cud. When it swallows again,

◀ These animals live on the African savanna. Each eats its own favorite kinds of plants.

Mouths That Adapt!

Black and white rhinos eat differently. The black rhino browses and grasps leaves with its pointed upper lip. The white rhino grazes and clips grass with its flat upper lip. ▼

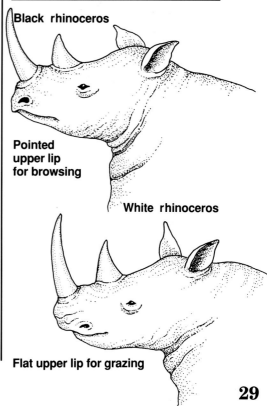

Black rhinoceros

Pointed upper lip for browsing

White rhinoceros

Flat upper lip for grazing

microscopic creatures finish the digestion of the plant material.

Grazers and Browsers

The herbivores shown above do not eat exactly the same plants, so the species do not compete for their food. Some graze on grass, others browse on leaves. Some animals do both.

Omnivores and Scavengers

Rats can live almost ▶ anywhere and eat almost anything — even candle wax and the plastic around wires! They can survive many different living conditions because of their eating habits.

Dung beetles eat dung, or animal feces. This dung ball will provide the beetle's family with food.▼

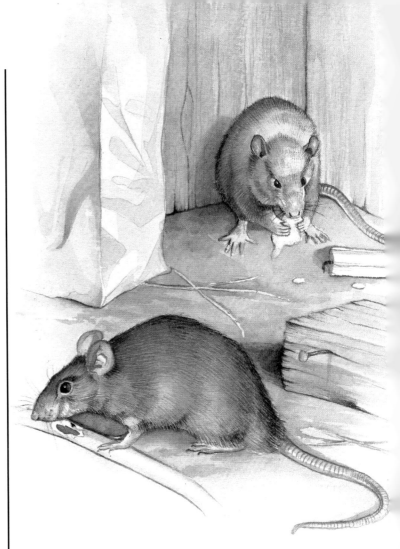

We call animals that eat plants and other animals omnivores.

Adaptable Omnivores

Eating many kinds of food can help animals survive. Rats are not choosy, and some foxes can live in the wild or in a city. In towns, foxes raid garbage cans for food.

Bears, pigs, blackbirds, and wasps are omnivores. Chimps

eat plants, fruit, and termites. They may even kill and eat baby baboons and antelope.

Scavengers

Many omnivores do not hunt for food, but eat rotting waste of plants or animals. We call these animals scavengers. They may even eat the dung, or feces, of other animals. Scavengers recycle natural materials back into the food cycle.

▲ Vultures feed off the bodies of dead animals.

Chimpanzees catch termites by dipping a twig into the termite nest.
▼

Specialist Feeders

Blood Meals

Some animals feed on the rich, nutritious blood of others. These animals include vampire bats, leeches, and mosquitoes. They are specially suited for feeding on blood. For example, a special chemical in their saliva stops the blood from forming clots. Blood clots stop a wound from bleeding.

Vampire bat

Sharp upper teeth (incisors)

Vampire bats use sharp ▶ teeth to bite their victims and have channels in their tongues for drinking the blood. They do not kill their victims directly. But they can carry and spread rabies.

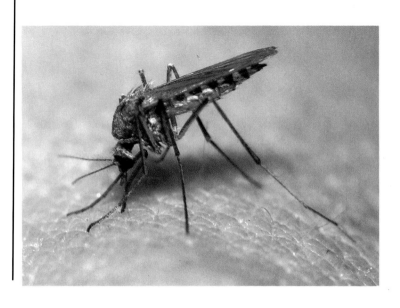

Female mosquitoes ▶ puncture the skin of their victims with a set of organs in the proboscis. Some mosquitoes carry malaria and other harmful diseases.

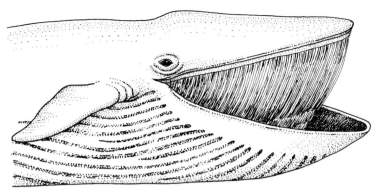

The whale's grooved throat works like an accordion and stretches out to take in lots of seawater.

Feeding by Filtering

Some animals filter their food out of water with special mouths. Microscopic animals called plankton live in the water in huge populations. Their tiny size means that the animal must take in a lot of water to get a whole meal.

The flamingo is a bird that strains its food through its beak.

Baleen whales are a group of whales that filter food through their mouths. The baleen, or whalebone, is attached to the upper jaw in the place of teeth. It forms a screen that catches millions of shrimplike krill with each mouthful.

◀ Baleen whales do not have teeth. They have instead a screen of whalebone that can be as long as 13 feet (4 m). The whalebone strains from the sea a meal of tiny animals.

Did You Know?

The rare giant panda lives in the bamboo forests of China. Its ancestors probably ate meat, but it only eats bamboo shoots now. In fact, the thumb evolved on each hand so it could grip the bamboo. These animals are now in danger. The bamboo forests are dying, and the pandas may not have enough to eat.
▼

How Not to Be Eaten

▲ These stick insects look like twigs on trees. They move very slowly and avoid the attention of possible predators.

The ptarmigan also has a way of blending in with its surroundings. ▶

There are many ways for animals to avoid being eaten by predators. One way, called camouflage, uses special colors or shapes to help the animal blend into its surroundings.

Safe Shells and Sharp Spines
Some animals have a hard shell or sharp spines to protect them. Armadillos have a thick skin that acts like a shell. A turtle pulls <u>into</u> its shell, and the porcupine has its many loose spines for protection.

A ptarmigan in summer plumage

Poisonous Protection

Some animals use venom to kill their prey or to protect themselves. Stingrays have venomous spines that help the venom enter the attacker's body.

Colorful Warnings

Some animals, such as bees, wasps, coral snakes, and skunks have striped patterns. These animals can be dangerous to other animals, and these warning colors are nature's way of telling predators to keep away!

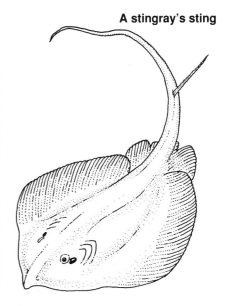

A stingray's sting

▲ The stingray has a venomous spine in its tail that it flicks out when threatened.

A ptarmigan in winter plumage

Clever Confusion

Sometimes an action, rather than a color or poison, saves an animal from attack. To escape, this lizard can break off its tail — and then grow a new one!

4: | THE SENSES

Animal Eyes

Animals have different kinds of eyes, some very simple, others more complex. Flatworms have very simple eyes. They see only light and dark. Insects have compound eyes made up of thousands of tubes. More tubes mean better vision.

Not all mammals can see colors the way we can. Antelope, dogs, and rodents see only black and white, or they see only a few colors. Many animals that <u>are</u> brightly colored <u>see</u> bright colors.

▲ Insects have eyes made of thousands of tiny tubes. This kind of eye is called a compound eye.

The eyes shown on both pages are from a bird. The first is shown as we see it, the other as a bee would see it. The bee's compound eye makes it see thousands of smaller, separate images. ▶

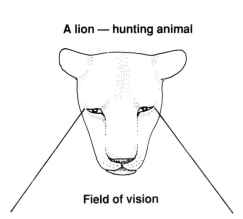

A lion — hunting animal

Field of vision

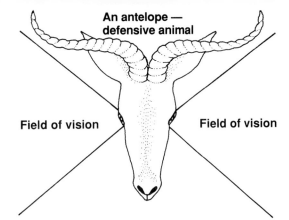

An antelope — defensive animal

Field of vision

Field of vision

Eyes for Life

Different kinds of animals have eyes in different places on their heads. We know an animal hunts if its eyes are on the front of its head, like a lion's eyes. If the eyes are on the side of the head, like an antelope's, it is a hunted animal. Lions need to judge distances; antelope need to see a wide area around them.

▲The lion has a narrow, focused field of vision. The antelope has a wide field of vision. These adaptations show the differences in how these animals live.

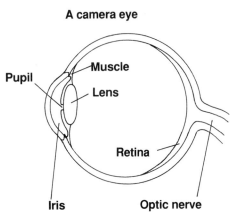

A camera eye

Pupil

Muscle

Lens

Retina

Iris

Optic nerve

▲Vertebrates have cameralike eyes. The pupil opens and closes to control how much light enters the eye. The lens helps focus, and the retina picks up the image of what is being looked at and sends it to the brain along the optic nerve.

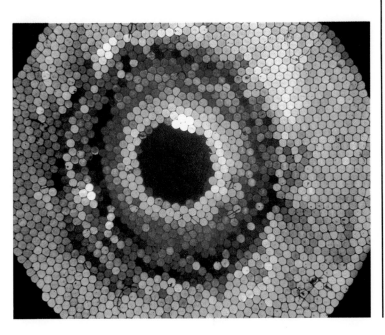

Smelling and Tasting

▲ The wolf's long, sensitive nose has bare, moist skin at the tip to help the wolf pick up distant smells.

Animals can pick up certain chemicals that float in the air or dissolve in water through the organs of smell and taste. The organs, called olfactory organs, are the nose and the tongue.

A World of Smells

The wolf's sense of smell is much stronger than a human's. The wolf can follow the trail of smells an animal has left. Sharks can smell the blood of an injured animal through 1/4 mile (0.4 km) of water.

Smelly Signals

Animal smells may be a message to other animals. The

Moths have large antennae to pick up smells from the air. ▶

This male lion has just picked up the scent of a female lion that is ready to mate. The female gives off special scents that attract mates and start the mating ritual.

signal that a female is ready to mate comes from the smell of a chemical called a pheromone. Male gypsy moths have large antennae that pick up the smell the female releases from 1 mile (1.6 km) away.

Spraying urine or leaving dung is usually a mark of territory. Special glands under the animal's tail or near the eye may also send out signals.

Did You Know?

When a snake flicks its tongue in and out, it is "tasting" the air. An organ called Jacobson's organ picks up smelly chemicals in the air and transmits the signals to the brain.

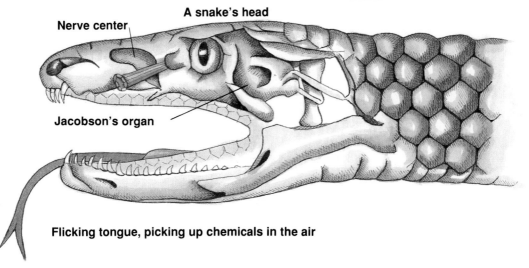

Nerve center

A snake's head

Jacobson's organ

Flicking tongue, picking up chemicals in the air

Hearing and Touch

Bush babies use their eyes and ears to detect food and danger. ▶

Bad Vibrations

Snakes do not have ears. They feel vibrations in the earth. So why do they rattle their tails if they cannot hear? They do it to warn hearing animals to keep away! ▼

Did You Know? ▶

Crickets have ears on their legs. Cicadas have ears at the base of their wings.

Hearing Is Important

Animals need hearing for both protection and survival. Nocturnal animals and animals living in forests have good hearing. They cannot see well in the dark or in trees, so they must listen for their enemies.

Ear flaps, or pinnae, help most mammals catch sounds. Seals and crocodiles live on land and in water, so their ear flaps close off their ears.

Cicada

Cricket

Area of body used for hearing

Sensitive Skin

Our bodies are sensitive to touch almost everywhere. Touch receptors make our fingers and tongue more sensitive than other parts of our bodies. Some mammals have whiskers that help them find their way in the dark. Otters and sea lions search for food with their whiskers.

These animals live on or near the seabed. The catfish has barbels that work like whiskers on its head. It can feel its way through cloudy water and taste things with its feelers. Lobsters and crabs do the same with their antennae. Gurnards have a pair of fins on the front of their bodies which they use to search for small animals in the sand.

Catfish

Lobster

Gurnard

Crab

The Sixth Sense

In addition to seeing, hearing, touching, smelling, and tasting, animals use other methods of sensing their world.

Shocking Senses

Some fish use electricity to find their way around. The electric eel sends out electric currents to sense its surroundings. It can produce five times as much voltage as a socket at home.

Lateral line (magnified)

Tiny hairs (pick up movement in the water)

Good Vibrations ▲

On fish and some amphibians, a lateral line runs along each side of the body. It is made of tiny cups filled with one small hair and slimy mucus. The hairs move with the flow of water, pick up vibrations, and let the animal know what is going on around it.

The electric eel gives off a powerful electrical current. The current can be used to stun attackers and prey. ▶

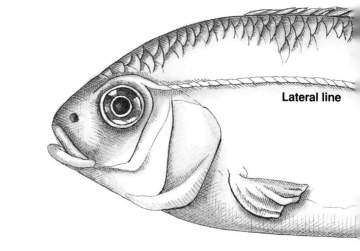

Lateral line

Electric eel

Electric current

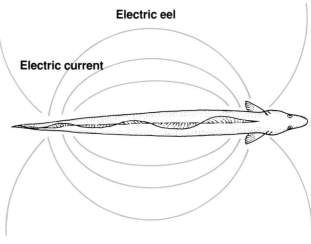

The Pope's pit viper has heat-sensitive pits between each eye and nostril. Thousands of temperature receptors pick up temperature changes that tell the snake there is another animal nearby. This is how pit vipers sense where their next meal is.

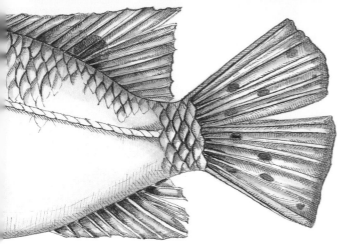

Seeing by Hearing

To find their way around and locate food, bats use echolocation — a high-pitched sound that bounces off objects and back to the bat's ears. This sense is important to bats, which are nocturnal and have poor eyesight.

▼

Heat Sensors

Rattlesnakes and other members of a group of snakes called vipers can sense the body heat of other animals. This sense allows them to catch prey in the dark.

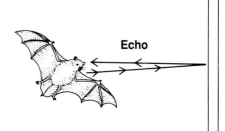

Echo

5: REPRODUCTION

How Animals Reproduce

Amoebas — Single-celled Creatures

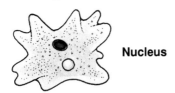

Nucleus

One amoeba

Two nuclei

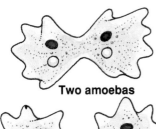

Two amoebas

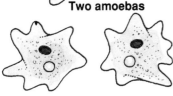

▲ The amoeba reproduces by dividing in two.

The human female carries an egg inside her, and the male's sperm fertilizes it. This leads to the growth of a baby inside the female. ▶

All animals must reproduce to continue their species. A single-celled creature like the amoeba divides in two. The hydra buds a new hydra off its own body. More complicated animals reproduce sexually.

Sexual Reproduction

Most animals are either male or female. The males' sex cells are sperm, and the females' sex cell is the egg. Fertilization occurs when a sperm enters an egg inside the female's body. A new cell is formed and divides again and again to form a new animal.

Some water animals, such as fish and frogs, fertilize outside their

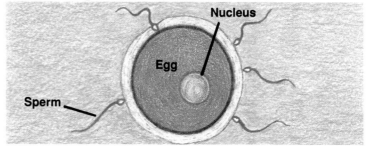

Nucleus

Egg

Sperm

bodies by releasing eggs and sperm into the water.

Eggs and Young

Birds and reptiles lay eggs. Inside the hard shell, the embryo, or developing young, is surrounded by its own food supply. When it is fully developed, it hatches. Young mammals are not in a shell, but feed through a placenta and an umbilical cord connected to the mother's stomach. The mother gives birth to the young.

◀ These lions are mating. The male's sperm will fertilize the female's egg in her womb. She will carry the developing cub inside her until it is ready to be born.

45

Finding a Mate

Amazing but True! ▶

In order to attract females, male bowerbirds decorate their nests with bright stones, feathers from other birds, and even buttons and bottle caps!

Showing Off

Bright colors are a common way of attracting a mate for many fish, amphibians, birds, and reptiles. The male peacock displays his bright tail feathers to show how strong and healthy he is. The female chooses the male with the most colorful plumage. During the mating season, the male green lizard displays his blue throat by bobbing his head up and down.

The feathers this peacock is displaying are meant to attract the female (peahen) for mating. ▼

Dancing Delights

Male and female cranes leap

46

into the air as part of their courtship dance. The male scorpion clasps his pincers onto the female's pincers and leads her in a kind of dance.

Animal Flashlights
Fireflies flash their lights to attract one another. Some deep-sea fish also use lights. The lights flash differently for different species.

To attract a mate, the male scorpion leads a dance, the male crested newt's belly turns red, and the male green lizard's throat turns blue. ▼

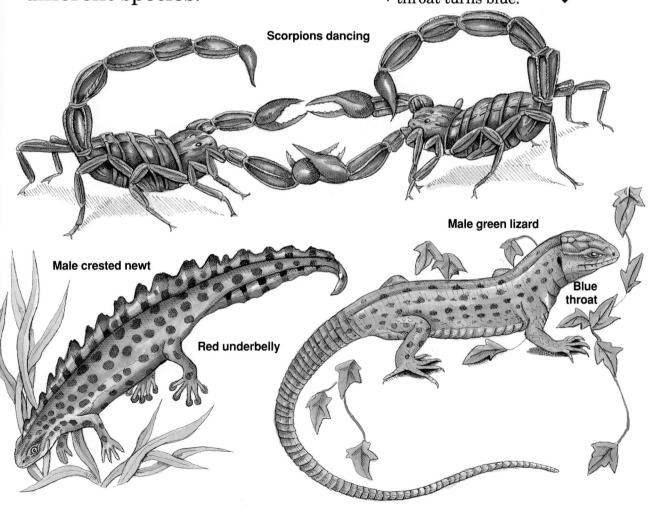

Scorpions dancing

Male green lizard

Blue throat

Male crested newt

Red underbelly

47

Animal Parents

Many animals, such as the codfish, show no interest in raising their young. But humans, scorpions, crocodiles, some fish, and many other animals spend a lot of time caring for their young.

The female orangutan spends lots of time caring for her baby. She will protect it and teach it how to survive. ▶

The male midwife toad keeps his eggs moist and safe from predators — by wrapping the eggs around his legs! ▼

Egg Protectors

Male giant water bugs carry eggs on their backs. Female shore crabs hide their eggs in a flap of hard shell under their bodies. Female wolf spiders carry a silk cocoon of eggs. These animals protect their eggs. They lay fewer eggs

When a baby kangaroo is born, it crawls into its mother's pouch. It will remain there until it grows stronger and can take care of itself. Animals with baby pouches are called marsupials. Other types of marsupials are wombats, bandicoots, and opossums.

than the codfish, since their eggs have a better chance of surviving.

Birds and Mammals

Some young animals care for themselves soon after being born. Pheasants and chickens feed as soon as they hatch. Only hours after birth, antelope and deer can walk with the herd.

Mammals feed their young on mother's milk. As the young grow, the mother helps them eat solid food. The mother koala feeds her young partly digested leaves in the form of dung, and soon they eat leaves from trees.

The female Nile crocodile keeps her newly hatched young safe from predators by putting them in a strange place — her mouth! This is called mouthbrooding.

Changing

Some animals are born in a form very different from their adult stage. The crab starts life as an egg and grows into a larva. From the larval stage, it changes into its adult form.

Adult mussels and barnacles are attached to ships and rocks. But their microscopic larvae float with the rest of the plankton.

The newly hatched flounder looks like any larval fish. But in the days that follow, one eye moves next to the other, the fish flips to one side so the eyes face up, and it then swims on its side.

Many sea animal larvae look very different from their adult parents. Here are a starfish and a crab with their larvae.
▼

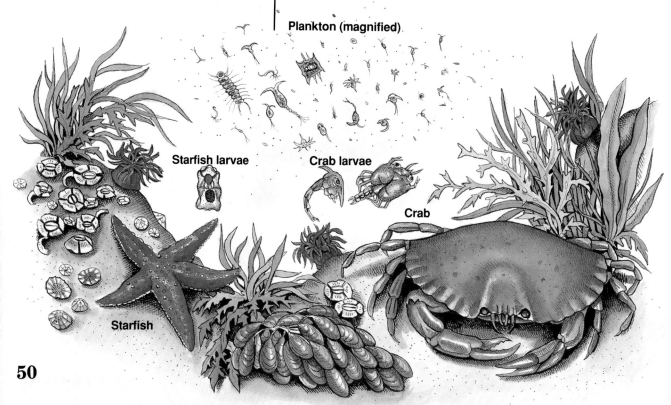

Plankton (magnified)

Starfish larvae

Crab larvae

Crab

Starfish

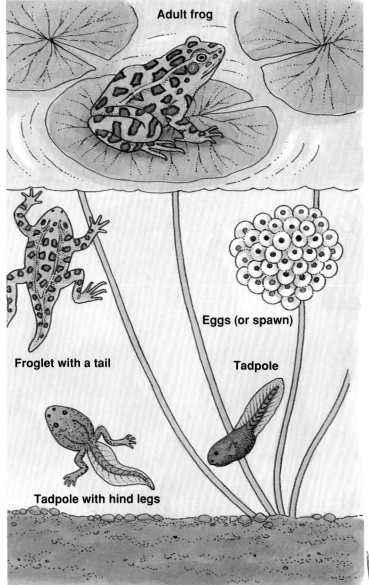

Adult frog

Froglet with a tail

Eggs (or spawn)

Tadpole

Tadpole with hind legs

A Different World

The dragonfly lays its eggs in water. As the larvae grow, they shed layers of skin. When their last layer of pupal skin is shed, they fly in search of a mate. The female mayfly must lay her eggs quickly, as adults live for only about a day!

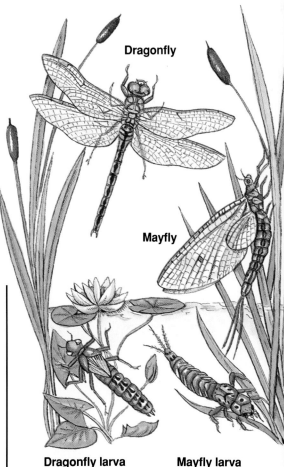

Dragonfly

Mayfly

Dragonfly larva

Mayfly larva

6: ANIMAL COMMUNITIES

Living Together

Most animals depend on their groups for survival. But some are solitary. The tiger lives alone in its own territory and will only join other members of its species at mating time.

Birds live and feed together in flocks. At night they join other flocks and roost together. Antelope live in a herd. They live in open spaces, and are much safer together than alone.

Predators live in groups, too. Wolves live in packs and help each other hunt and kill larger animals, like moose.

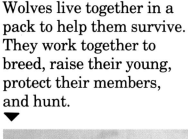

Wolves live together in a pack to help them survive. They work together to breed, raise their young, protect their members, and hunt.

Breeding Groups

Northern elephant seals spend most of their lives out at sea. But at breeding time, they gather on beaches in California and Mexico. The males fight to breed with the females, and the females return to sea when their calves are born. Male deer also fight over females. After the breeding season, the females and young live with one male, while the other males form a group of their own.

▲ Many animals of the African plain live in large herds. Impalas, zebras, and wildebeests all find safety in numbers.

These female northern elephant seals are in a breeding group. ▼

Animal Colonies

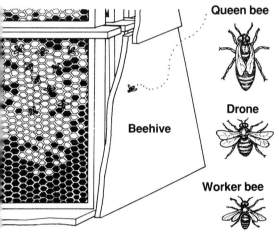

Queen bee

Beehive

Drone

Worker bee

▲ Three types of bees and their home, the hive.

Some species live in groups where each member depends on the group for survival.

Naked Mole Rats
In Africa, colonies of naked mole rats tunnel underground for food. They pass dirt back until the last one in line throws it out on the surface. The rat at the end warns the others of danger, so even if that rat is eaten by a snake, the colony will survive.

Queens in Control
Bees, wasps, and ants live in colonies. Honeybee colonies are

Baboons have well-ordered groups. The dominant male protects the group from attack. The younger males help the dominant one. They all groom each other.

▶

This coral colony is made up of thousands of tiny animals called polyps.

The Portuguese Man-of-War

The man-of-war is really a colony of many polyps. Each polyp has a job to do. Some polyps form tentacles. Some make up the parts that reproduce. The float acts like a sail. Each polyp depends on the others for its survival.

made up of three kinds of bee. The queen bee lays eggs and controls the colony. Male drones mate with queen bees. Worker bees collect food, feed the colony, and raise the young.

In some ant colonies, soldier ants defend the colony and often die for it.

Coral Colonies

Many very tiny animals, called polyps, share food with each other and connect to each other to form a coral colony.

Animal Partners

Sometimes different species form partnerships. Some partnerships help both partners, while some help only one.

Friends Helping Friends
Ants and aphids help each other. The aphids produce a milky honeydew that ants like to eat. In return for their food, ants fight off aphid enemies, such as the ladybug.

Corals are sea animals that depend on tiny plants, called algae, for growth. Algae grow inside the coral and increase the speed of growth of the chalky coral skeletons. Also in the sea, tiny fish called cleaner wrasse clean off dead skin and small parasites from other fish. They get food; the other fish get clean.

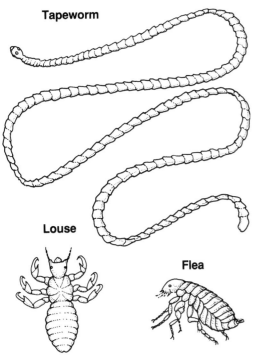

Tapeworm

Louse

Flea

▲ These parasites live on or in the body of another animal. They feed off the food that their host animal eats.

Ants "milk" these aphids for food. In return, the ants protect the aphids from enemies.

▶

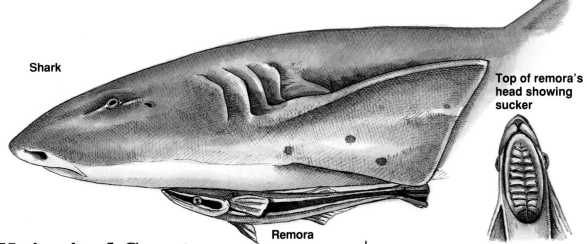

Shark

Remora

Top of remora's head showing sucker

Uninvited Guests

Some animals take free food or protection for nothing in return. The colorful clownfish hides among the sea anemone's deadly tentacles to escape its enemies and pick up the anemone's food scraps. Remoras attach themselves to sharks, get a free ride, and eat the shark's food scraps. A species of ragworm lives in the shell of the hermit crab and eats some of the food that the crab finds. And what about the crab? It gets nothing in return.

▲ The remora attaches itself to the underside of sharks with a special fin. This fin acts like a sucker. The remora rides along and eats food scraps from the shark. The picture above shows the sucker on top of the remora's head.

◀ These clownfish hide safely among the deadly tentacles of the giant sea anemone. While the tentacles do not harm the clownfish, they do keep predators away.

Sending Messages

These butterfly fish have similar markings so they can recognize one another. ▶

▲ The white-tail deer flags its tail as a warning of danger.

Every killer whale has unique markings, just as humans have fingerprints. ▼

Besides humans, whales and dolphins are among the few kinds of animals that use talking as a form of communication. Other animals must find other ways to communicate.

Who Are You?

Members of one species are often marked similarly for easy recognition. Some species have slightly different pattern marks, so each member looks a bit different. Groups of monkeys

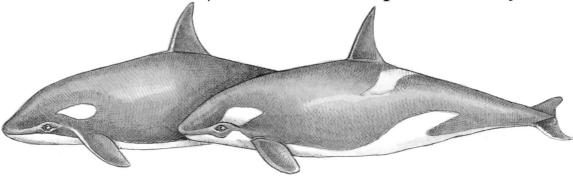

always have leaders. The leading male mandrill can be easily recognized by his bright blue and red face.

Mood Signals

When an animal's mood changes, something about its appearance may change, too. Monkeys can change their facial expression with each mood. A male monkey may yawn and show his teeth to signal that he is threatening another monkey in the troop. If the other monkey does not behave itself and try to calm down the male monkey, it may be in trouble.

▲The mandrill is a Western African baboon. This male has a brightly colored face, which means he is a leader.

Territory

Animals communicate the boundaries of their territory. Birds sing, gibbons shout, cats spray urine, and lizards bob their heads and display their colors. These signals warn other animals to stay away.

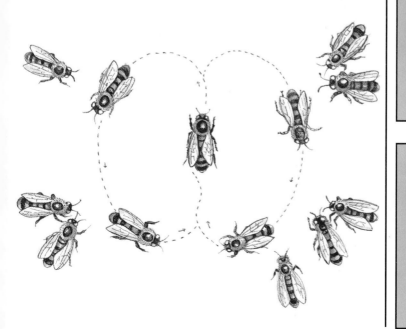

◄ Spreading the News

Bees communicate to the rest of their group where they have found food. They dance and wiggle in a combination of signals that tells the location and distance of the food.

Glossary

Adapted: Suited to live a particular way of life.

Amoeba: A tiny, single-celled animal that changes shape as it moves.

Ancestor: A relative who was alive in the past.

Antennae: Long structures on or near the head of some animals that can be used to touch, taste, and even smell.

Aquatic mammal: A mammal that lives in water, such as a dolphin or a whale.

Baleen: Whalebone; elastic, hornlike material made from the same material as hair and fingernails that hangs from the top of some whales' mouths and is used for filtering out tiny animals from the water.

Barbels: Fleshy "whiskers" found on some fish that can touch, taste, and smell.

Biologist: A scientist who studies living things, such as plants and animals.

Camouflage: The use of colors, patterns, and shapes to help animals stay hidden against a specific background.

Canine teeth: Teeth found in most mammals. They are long and daggerlike in cats and dogs, and short but pointed in humans.

Carbon dioxide: A gas produced when animals breathe. It is formed from carbon and oxygen.

Clot: To clump together to become more solid than liquid, such as when blood clots to stop a cut from bleeding.

Communication: The exchange of information between two or more individuals.

Compete: In the case of animals, to struggle for limited food, space, and mates.

Compound eye: An eye made up of many smaller simple parts, each with its own lens.

Density: How much something weighs for its size. Water is denser than air because if the same amount of air and water were weighed, water would weigh much more than air.

Diffusion: The movement of gases or liquids from an area of high concentration to an area of low concentration.

Digestion: The process by which food is broken down into a form that can be taken up into the rest of the body.

Dissolve: To change from a solid or gas into a liquid.

Echidna: A kind of spiny anteater from Australia and New Guinea.

Echolocation: The ability of an animal to use sound to find its way around.

Egg: The female sex cell.

Embryo: An early stage in the development of an animal, just after the stage of the egg cell.

Energy: The force or power used to move things or do other work. There are many kinds of energy, such as heat, light, sound, and chemical and nuclear energy.

Evolve: To change gradually, over long periods of time.

Extinct: In the case of living things, no longer existing in living form.

Fertilization: The joining of male and female sex cells to create a unified cell.

Flatworm: A simple organism found in water.

Focus: A point at which light rays meet to give a clear image of an object.

Fossilization: What happens when the hard parts dead animals become preserved in rocks.

Genus: A group of closely related animals that contains several species.

Gestation: The length of time from fertilization unt birth.

Gills: Parts of the body used by certain water animals, such as fish, for taking oxygen from the water.

Herbivores: Animals that eat only plants or parts plants such as fruit, seeds, and nectar.

Hermit crab: A kind of crab that lives in the shell o another animal, like a snail, for protection.

Hibernation: Spending the winter sleeping, as som animals do.

Honeydew: Sugary fluid made by insects.

Hydra: A tiny polyp with a tube-shaped body and a mouth ringed with tentacles.

Incubate: To keep eggs warm for hatching.

Invertebrate: An animal that has no backbone.

Jet propulsion: A way of moving using a backward force to push forward.

Krill: Small shrimplike animals found in such enormous numbers that they are the food of many animals in the ocean, including whales.

Larva: An early stage of some animals' development It looks different from the adult. Caterpillars and grubs are insect larvae.

Lateral line: A sense organ in fish and some amphibians used to detect vibrations.

Lens: A clear object that is curved to bend light rays passing through it.

Malaria: A disease caused by a single-celled organism called *Plasmodium* which is carried by mosquitoes.

Mandrill: A type of monkey from Africa.

Membrane: A thin layer of material that lines or covers a part of the body.

Microscopic: Something that is so small it can only be seen with a microscope.

Migrate: To move regularly from one area to another

Mouthbrooding: In the case of some animals (mainly fish), protecting the eggs and young by keeping them safe in the parents' mouths.

Mucus: Slimy substance produced in or on an animal's body.

Network: An interweaving system.

Nocturnal: A word used to describe animals that are active at night.

Nutritious: In the case of food, rich in goodness and energy.

Olfactory: Concerned with the sense of smell.

Omnivores: Animals that eat both plants and animals.

Opposable: Capable of being placed opposite something. For example, the thumb is an opposable digit on the human hand.

Oxygen: A gas that nearly all living things breathe. It is found in air and water.

Parasite: A plant or animal living in or on a different kind of plant or animal that gets its food from that plant or animal.

Pectoral: Having to do with the chest.

Pelvic bone: A bone in the lower part of a vertebrate's body.

Pheromone: A chemical made by an animal which, when released, acts as a signal for another individual of the same species.

Pinna (*plural:* pinnae): The ear flap of skin found only in mammals.

Placenta: An organ attached to a developing mammal inside its mother's uterus. The placenta helps bring nourishment to the developing mammal from its mother.

Plankton: The name given to the many tiny and microscopic plants and animals that drift with the tides and currents in the seas.

Polyp: A tube-shaped animal with a ring of tentacles around its mouth.

Predator: Any animal that kills other animals for food, such as a lion.

Prehensile: Adapted for gripping or holding, like a spider monkey's tail.

Prey: Any animal that becomes the food of another, like an antelope eaten by a lion.

Proboscis: In some animals, the long part of a mouth used in feeding, such as a butterfly's sucking organ or an elephant's trunk.

Pupal: At the stage of an insect's development when it is changing from a larva into an adult. An insect at the pupal stage is protected by a covering such as a cocoon.

Pupil: Opening in the front of the eye through which light enters.

Rabies: A deadly disease passed from animal to animal by biting.

Radar: A device for finding the distance and measuring the speed of a distant object by bouncing radio waves off it.

Ragworm: A kind of worm that lives in the mud and sand of the seashore.

Recycle: To treat substances or materials that have been thrown away, such as newspapers, glass, or cans, so they can be used again.

Remora: A fish that has a special sucker on its head for attaching itself to sharks and other animals.

Reproduction: The process of making new individuals of a species.

Retina: A light-sensitive layer of cells at the back of the eye.

Roost: A place where birds rest.

Saliva: A liquid substance made in the mouth of mammals that helps digestion.

Scavengers: Animals that eat dead or rotting plant and animal life.

Sexual: Having to do with the two groups, male and female, into which many living things are divided.

Sheath: A thin outer covering that surrounds and protects.

Solitary: Living alone.

Species: A group of animals so closely related that they can breed with each other.

Sperm: Male sex cells.

Spiracles: The holes in the sides of an insect's body used for breathing.

Streamlined: Curved in order to move easily through water or air.

Temperature receptor: A tiny sense organ lying in the skin of animals that reacts to temperature.

Tentacles: Narrow, flexible body parts that help certain animals move or grasp things.

Territory: An area where an animal or group of animals lives which they will defend as their own against other members of the same species.

Touch receptor: A tiny sense organ lying in the skin of animals that reacts to being touched.

Umbilical cord: In certain animals, the flexible, cordlike structure connecting the developing young to its mother.

Urine: Fluid made by animals to remove waste products from the body.

Vegetation: Plant life.

Venom: A special poisonous liquid used by many different animals to kill their prey or defend themselves from attackers.

Venomous: Containing or making poison; poisonous.

Warning colors: The bright colors on certain poisonous animals that warn other animals they are dangerous.

Womb: The uterus; the place where a young mammal grows inside its mother.

Index

A **boldface** number shows
that the entry is illustrated on
that page. The same page often
has text about the entry, too.